ANIMALS
That Make a Difference!

Llamas

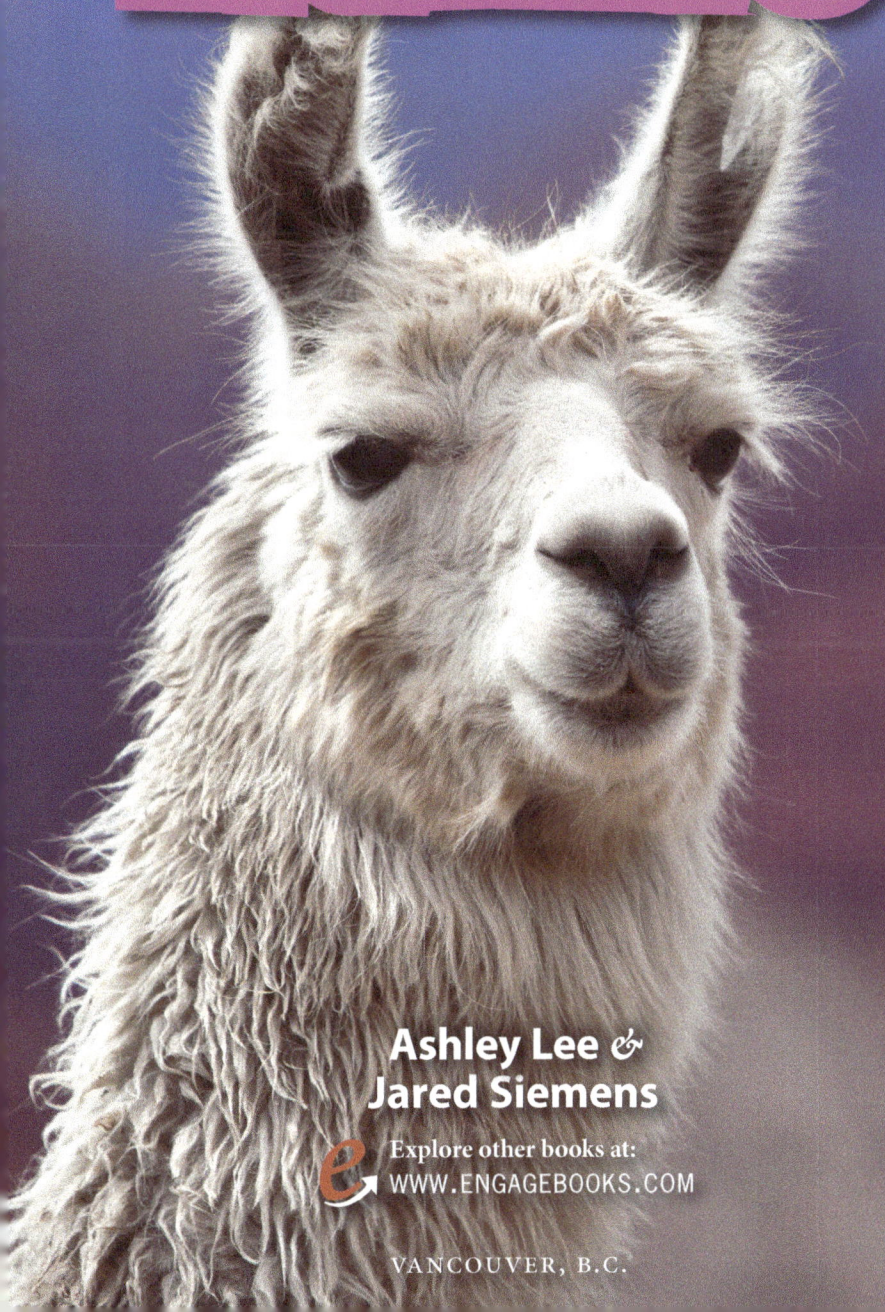

Ashley Lee & Jared Siemens

e Explore other books at:
WWW.ENGAGEBOOKS.COM

VANCOUVER, B.C.

WWW.ENGAGEBOOKS.COM

Llamas: Level 2
Animals That Make a Difference!
Lee, Ashley 1995 –
Siemens, Jared 1989 –
Text © 2020 Engage Books
Design © 2020 Engage Books

Edited by: A.R. Roumanis and Lauren Dick
Design by: A.R. Roumanis

Text set in Arial Regular.
Chapter headings set in Arial Black.

FIRST EDITION / FIRST PRINTING

LIBRARY AND ARCHIVES CANADA CATALOGUING IN PUBLICATION

Title: Llamas: Animals That Make a Difference Level 2 reader / Ashley Lee, Jared
Siemens
Names: Lee, Ashley, author. Siemens, Jared, author.

Identifiers: Canadiana (print) 20200309048 | Canadiana (ebook) 20200309056
ISBN 978-1-77437-651-5 (hardcover)
ISBN 978-1-77437-652-2 (softcover)
ISBN 978-1-77437-653-9 (pdf)
ISBN 978-1-77437-654-6 (epub)
ISBN 978-1-77437-655-3 (kindle)

Subjects:
LCSH: Llamas—Juvenile literature
LCSH: Human-animal relationships—Juvenile literature.

Classification: LCC QL737.U54 S54 2020 | DDC J599.63/67—DC23

Contents

3

What Are Llamas?

Llamas are mammals. Mammals are animals with warm blood and a **backbone**.

Llamas are very helpful to people, other animals, and Earth.

KEY WORD

backbone: a row of bones that runs along the center of the back.

Llamas are part of the camel family, but they do not have a hump like a camel.

A Closer Look

Llamas have long necks.
A full-grown llama is about
6 feet (1.2 meters) tall.
This is about as tall
as an adult human.

Llamas are covered
in very soft wool. It
is most often brown,
black, or white
in color.

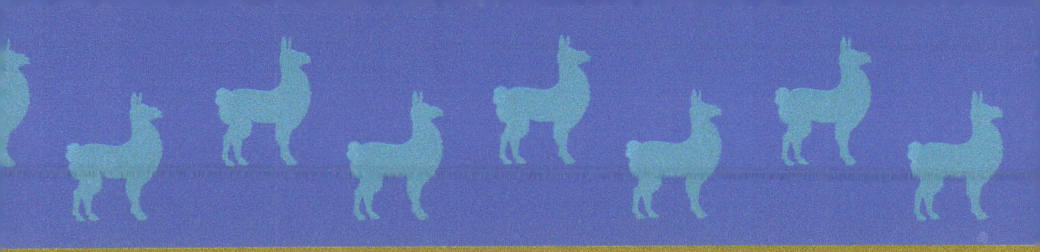

Llamas have long, banana-shaped ears.

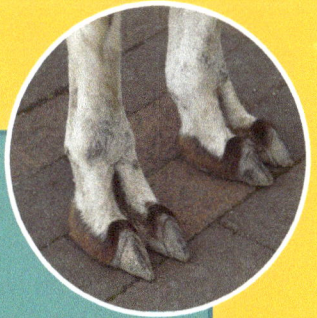

Llamas have two padded toes on each foot. These toes are covered in hard nails.

Where Do Llamas Live?

Llamas were first found in cold mountain and grassland places in South America. **Indigenous** people in South America raised llamas to help with their tasks.

Llamas are found mostly in Bolivia, Chile, and Peru. Today, many people all over the world keep them on their farms.

Arctic Ocean

Atlantic Ocean

Europe

North America

Africa

Pacific Ocean

Peru

South America

Bolivia

Chile

Southern Ocean

Legend
Land
Ocean

0   2,000 miles
0   4,000 kilometers

N

What Do Llamas Eat?

Llamas eat mostly grass, lichens, and small shrubs. They also like flowering plants and tree leaves.

Llamas that live on farms eat food made for horses, sheep, and goats. This includes grains and hay.

Llamas eat about 11 pounds (5 kilograms) of food a day.

How Do Llamas Talk to Each Other?

A mother llama sometimes hums to help her babies know she is there.

A scared or surprised llama will make a kind of squeaky laughing sound.

An angry llama
may make a high-
pitch scream.

Llamas may be
upset if their ears
are back. A llama
is probably happy
and relaxed if its
ears are up.

13

Llama Life Cycle

Llamas have three stages in their life cycle. Baby llamas are called crias. Crias need to drink milk often as they grow.

Crias can walk 5 minutes after they are born.

Crias weigh up to 35 pounds (16 kg). They stop drinking their mother's milk when they are about 6 months old. When llamas reach about 3 years old, they are adults. A healthy llama can live as long as 30 years.

A full-grown llama weighs between 280 and 450 pounds (136 and 204 kg).

Curious Facts About Llamas

A llama's back legs give off a special smell. These smells help llamas tell each other apart.

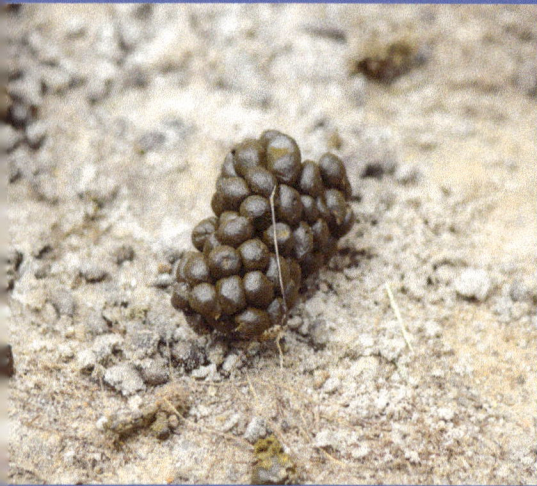

Llama poop has almost no smell.

A llama may stick its tongue out when it is not happy.

Llamas can be very stubborn. If a load on their back is too heavy, they won't move until it is made lighter.

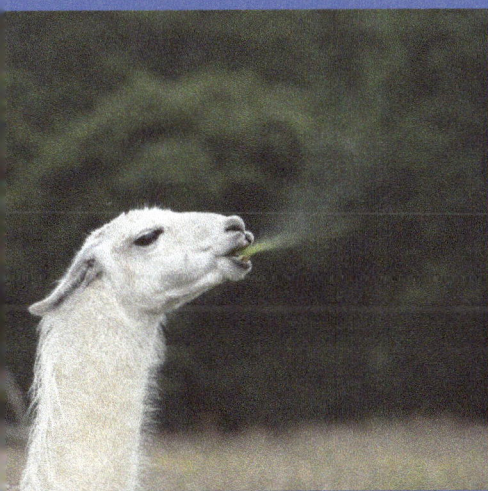

Llamas may spit when they are upset. They can spray their spit up to 15 feet (5 meters) away.

Llamas can run up to 40 miles (64 kilometers) per hour.

Part of the Llama Family

Llamas are part of a family of animals called camelids. They all have two toes on each foot. Four other animals are part of this family.

Vicuñas are the smallest animals in the family. They also have a mane of fur on their chests.

Alpacas are smaller than llamas and have shorter ears.

Camels may have one or two humps on their backs.

Guanacos are the only wild species of the camelid family. They have brown backs, white bellies, and long pointy ears.

19

How Llamas Help Other Animals

Llamas can become friends with other animals. They will keep sheep or other farm animals safe from danger.

Llamas can tell the difference between a friendly dog and a hungry coyote. A llama may spit or charge if it senses danger.

How Llamas Help Earth

Llamas help Earth by eating weeds and plants that can hurt other plants. By eating these plants, Llamas help good plants to grow.

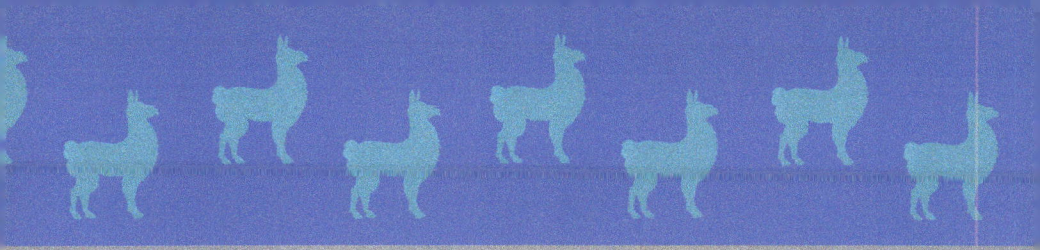

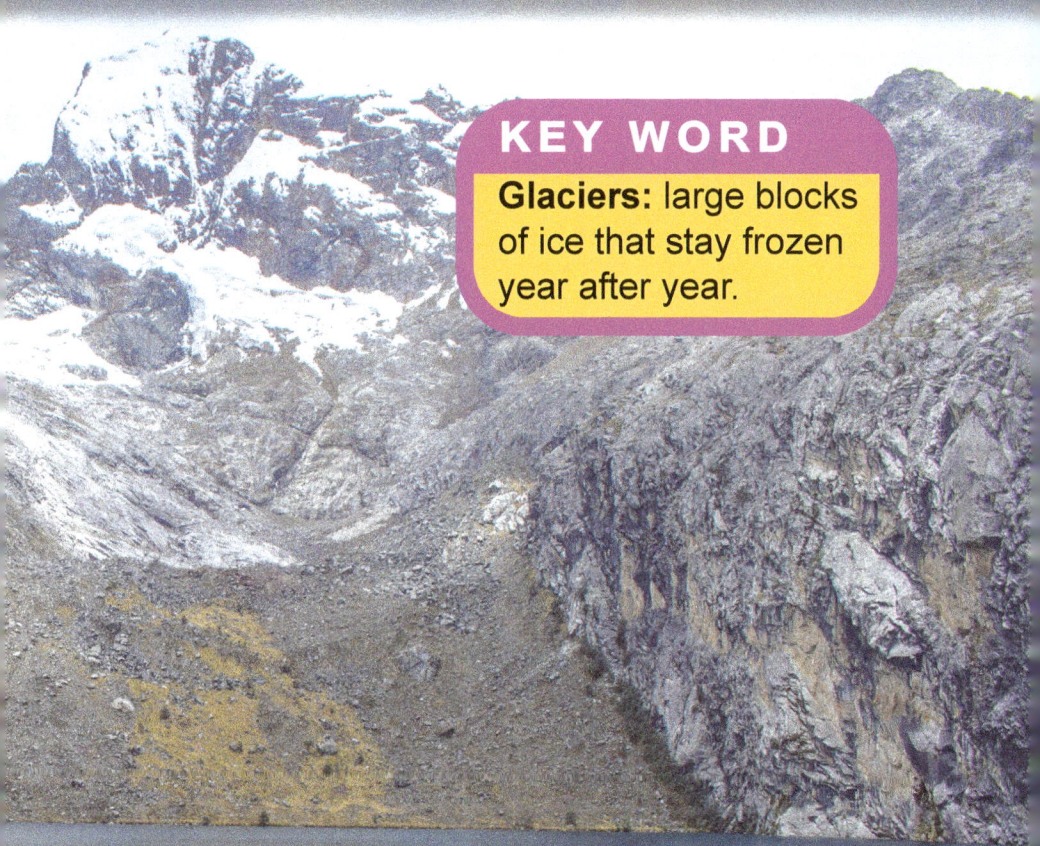

As Earth warms, mountain **glaciers** are melting. It is difficult for new plants to grow in the left over soil. Llama poop spreads plant seeds to these places and helps make the soil healthy.

How Llamas Help Humans

Humans use soft llama wool to make clothes, blankets, rugs, and rope.

Llamas can make up to 6 pounds (3 kg) of fleece every 2 years.

People from the Andes Mountains use llamas to help them carry heavy loads.

A llama can carry up to 132 pounds (60 kg) about 18.6 miles (30 km) in a single day.

Llama Family in Danger

People once hunted vicuñas and guanacos for food and wool. They hunted until there were very few left. When there are very few of an animal left, it is called endangered.

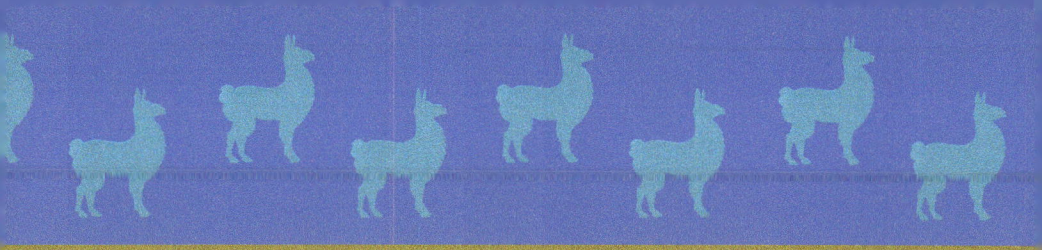

Vicuñas and guanacos are protected in many countries now. Their numbers are increasing. Neither animal is endangered any more.

How To Help Llamas

The climate in Peru is changing. This makes the summers and winters much colder. The colder weather kills the plants that llamas eat. Many llamas are dying because they cannot find food.

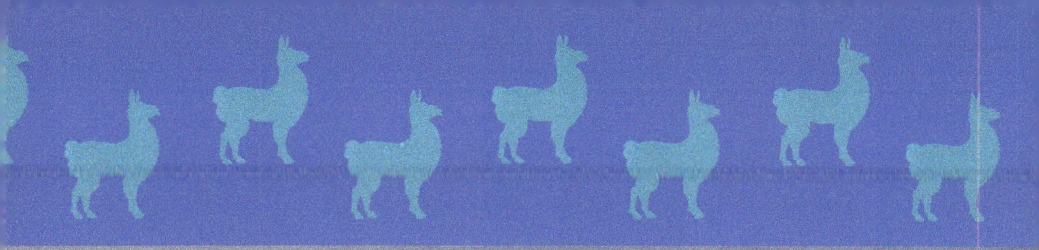

People can help llamas. We can pay farmers a fair price for wool clothing. This will help farmers buy enough food for their llamas.

Quiz

Test your knowledge of llamas by answering the following questions. The questions are based on what you have read in this book. The answers are listed on the bottom of the next page.

1 What are baby llamas called?

2 What does it mean when a llama sticks its tongue out?

3 How many animals are part of the llama family?

4 What will a llama do if it senses danger?

5 How do llamas help Earth?

6 Why are many llamas dying?

Explore other books in the Animals That Make a Difference series.

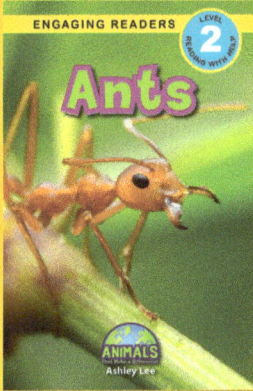

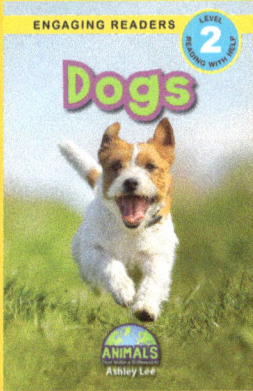

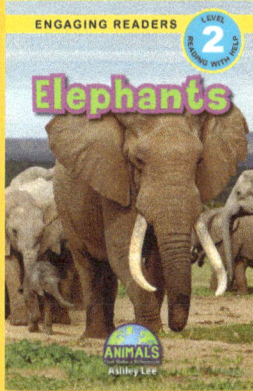

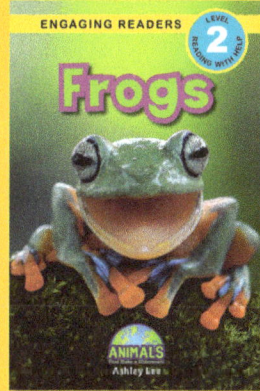

ENGAGING READERS — LEVEL 2 — READING WITH HELP
Ants
ANIMALS That Make a Difference
Ashley Lee

ENGAGING READERS — LEVEL 2 — READING WITH HELP
Beavers
ANIMALS That Make a Difference
Ashley Lee

ENGAGING READERS — LEVEL 2 — READING WITH HELP
Butterflies
ANIMALS That Make a Difference
Ashley Lee

ENGAGING READERS — LEVEL 2 — READING WITH HELP
Dogs
ANIMALS That Make a Difference
Ashley Lee

ENGAGING READERS — LEVEL 2 — READING WITH HELP
Elephants
ANIMALS That Make a Difference
Ashley Lee

ENGAGING READERS — LEVEL 2 — READING WITH HELP
Frogs
ANIMALS That Make a Difference
Ashley Lee

ENGAGING READERS — LEVEL 2 — READING WITH HELP
Llamas
ANIMALS That Make a Difference
Ashley Lee & Jared Siemens

ENGAGING READERS — LEVEL 2 — READING WITH HELP
Octopuses
ANIMALS That Make a Difference
Ashley Lee

ENGAGING READERS — LEVEL 2 — READING WITH HELP
Primates
ANIMALS That Make a Difference
Ashley Lee

Visit www.engagebooks.com to explore more Engaging Readers.

Answers:
1. Crias 2. It is not happy 3. Four 4. Spit or charge 5. By eating weeds and plants that can hurt other plants 6. They cannot find food

31

www.ingramcontent.com/pod-product-compliance
Lightning Source LLC
Chambersburg PA
CBHW051238020426
42331CB00016B/3430